Livonia Public Library
CIVIC CENTER #32
32777 Five Mile Road
Livonia, Michigan 48154
734.466.2491

Henry Goes to School

A Book about School Community

by Meg Gaertner

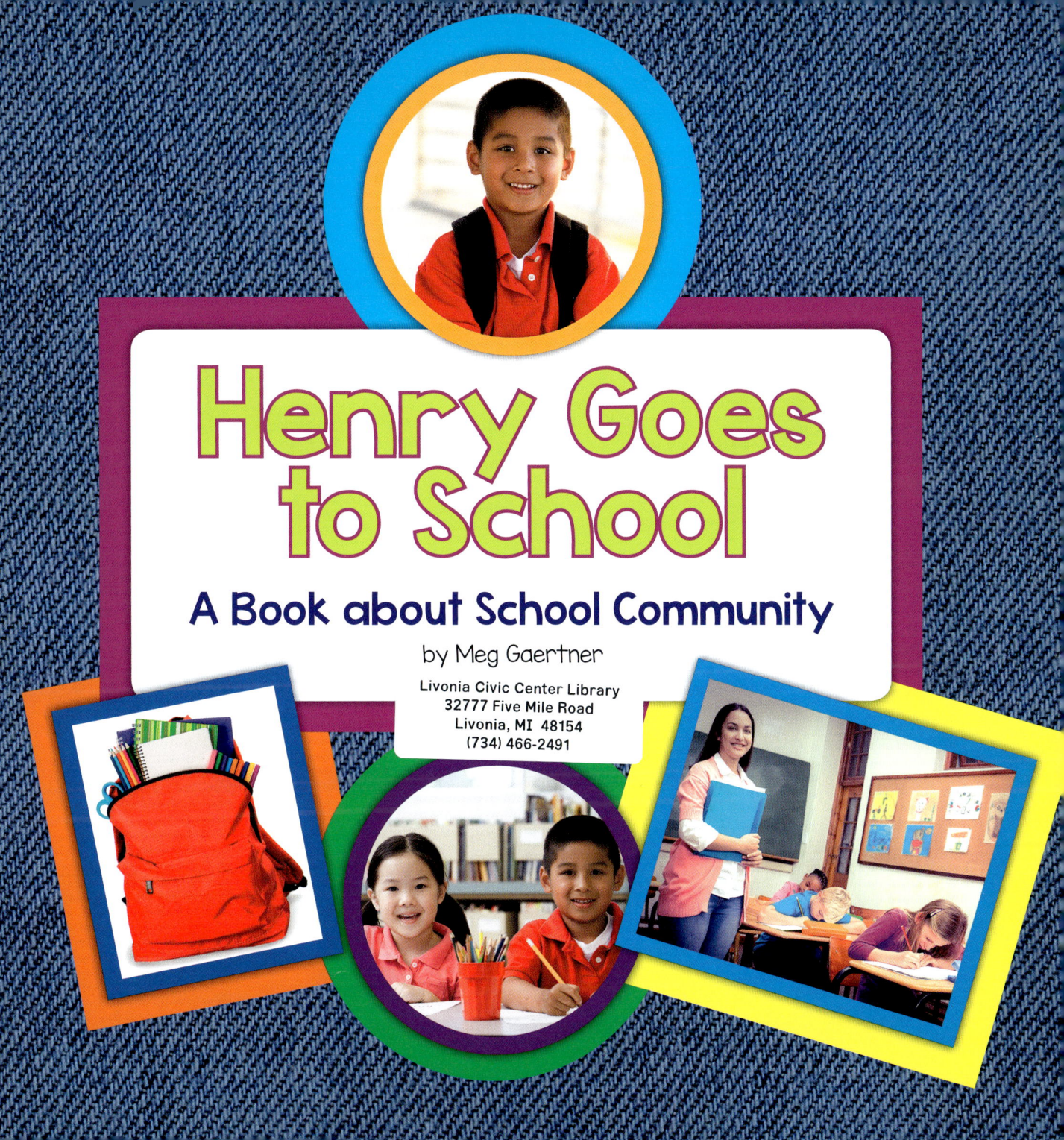

Published by The Child's World®
1980 Lookout Drive • Mankato, MN 56003-1705
800-599-READ • www.childsworld.com

Photographs ©: Monkey Business Images/Shutterstock Images, cover (top), cover (bottom middle), 1 (top), 1 (bottom middle), 3, 4, 13, 14, 18, 21; Shutterstock Images, cover (bottom left), 1 (bottom left); Wave Break Media/Shutterstock Images, cover (bottom right), 1 (bottom right); Monkey Business Images/iStockphoto, 7; iStockphoto, 8; Brian Eichhorn/Shutterstock Images, 10; Fang Xia Nuo/iStockphoto, 17

Copyright © 2019 by The Child's World®
All rights reserved. No part of the book may be reproduced or utilized in any form or by any means without written permission from the publisher.

ISBN HARDCOVER: 9781503827554
ISBN PAPERBACK: 9781622434275
LCCN: 2017964160

Printed in the United States of America • PA02388

About the Author

Meg Gaertner is a children's book author and editor who lives in Minnesota. When not writing, she enjoys dancing and spending time outdoors.

Today was a big day for Henry.
What happened to Henry today?

Henry went to school! He saw all of his friends.

The **principal** greeted them. The principal is the school's leader. She makes sure school is safe and fun.

Henry met his **homeroom** teacher. He teaches subjects like math and reading.

10

Henry passed the nurse's office. The nurse makes sure students stay healthy.

At lunch, servers gave food to students who did not bring their own.

Henry went to art class.
His art teacher helped him paint a picture.

Henry passed the **custodian**. The custodian keeps the school clean.

The day flew by so fast!
Henry loved going to school!

Who are the people in your school community?

Glossary

custodian (kuhss-TOH-dee-uhn) A custodian is someone who takes care of and cleans a large building. Henry saw a custodian sweeping the floor at school.

homeroom (HOME-room) The homeroom is the classroom in which students meet their teacher at the beginning of the school day. Henry's homeroom teacher took attendance and read announcements.

principal (PRIN-suh-puhl) A principal is the leader of a school. Emma's mom called the principal's office when Emma was sick and had to stay home from school.

Extended Learning Activities

1. Have you met your school's principal? How does he or she help the school's community?

2. Is your school big or small? Do you have a lot of people in your school community?

3. Henry has teachers who teach art, math, and reading. What are your favorite classes?

To Learn More

Books

Blake, Rose. *Going to School*.
London, UK: Frances Lincoln Children's Books, 2018.

Kalman, Bobbie. *My School Community*.
New York, NY: Crabtree Publishing, 2010.

McNiven, Lauren. *Schools in Different Places*.
New York, NY: Crabtree Publishing, 2016.

Web Sites

Visit our Web site for links about school community:
childsworld.com/links

Note to Parents, Teachers, and Librarians: We routinely verify our Web links to make sure they are safe, active sites—so encourage your readers to check them out!